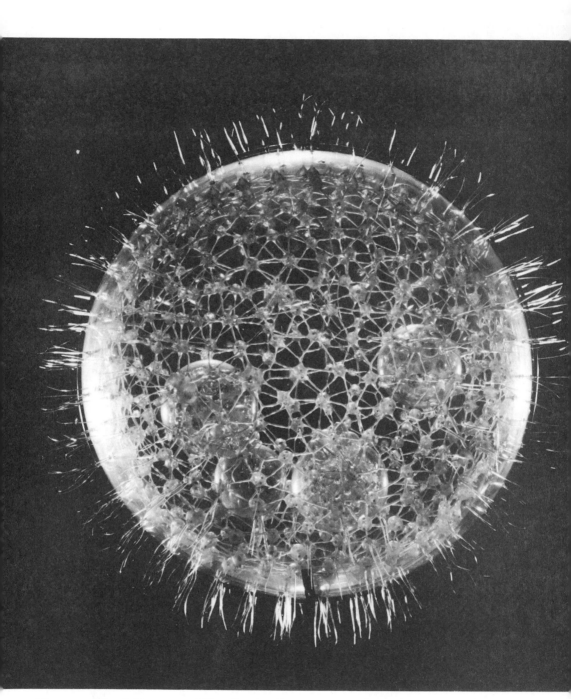

Glass model of Protozoa (Flagellata). Courtesy American Museum of Natural History.

A
World
in a
Drop of Water

Exploring with a Microscope

Alvin and Virginia Silverstein

DOVER PUBLICATIONS, INC.
Mineola, New York

Bibliographical Note

This Dover edition, first published in 1998 is an unabridged republica-
tion of the work originally published by Atheneum, New York in 1969.

Library of Congress Cataloging-in-Publication Data

Silverstein, Alvin.
    A world in a drop of water : exploring with a microscope / Alvin and
Virginia Silverstein.
        p.   cm.
    Originally published: 1st ed. New York : Atheneum, 1969.
    Includes index.
    Summary: Describes the structure and characteristics of the amoe-
ba, paramecium, and other members of the "circus" that Leeuwenhoek
discovered in a drop of water.
    ISBN 0-486-40381-5 (pbk.)
    1. Freshwater biology—Juvenile literature.   [1. Freshwater biolo-
gy.]   I. Silverstein, Virginia B.   II. Title.
QH96.16.S55   1998
578.76—dc21   98-27926
                                                           CIP
                                                           AC

Manufactured in the United States of America
Dover Publications, Inc., 31 East 2nd Street, Mineola, N.Y. 11501

Contents

A
World
in a
Drop of Water

Let's Go Hunting

LET'S GO OUT HUNTING! What shall we hunt for? Lions and tigers? Of course not! We wouldn't be able to find any *real* lions and tigers nearby (except in the zoo). We could hunt butterflies or grasshoppers or frogs. But let's try something more exciting this time. Let's go after some stranger game.

How about a creature that can squeeze in and out like an accordion and has two whirling wheels on top of its head? And another that looks like a blob of jelly, which can change its shape and send out snakelike arms to catch its prey? How about a green-speckled creature that darts about with a lashing, whiplike tail?

Do they sound as if they came from another world? Where can we find them? How can we catch them? Will it be dangerous?

Pond with scum (Pennsylvania). Photo by Ralph Buchsbaum.

They live closer than you think. And the strange monsters that we seek will not hurt you at all, no matter how fierce they look.

For our hunting expedition, no special equipment will be needed at first. Just bring along a few jars. Ordinary glass jars will do.

We are going to a nearby pond. For the strange "big game" that we are hunting is not really big at all. In fact, our "monsters" are to be found in every pond, large and small. If we know how to look for them, we can find them, swimming and floating and creeping in any pond.

At the pond we find that a velvet green moss makes a soft mat along the edge. Tall grassy weeds grow up through the quiet water. The top of the water is covered with a thin coat of green. Suddenly there is a big splash. A frog that was sunning itself on a rock must

Green frog. Courtesy American Museum of Natural History.

4

have heard us coming. As the ripples die away, we can see through the hole that he tore in the thin green coverlet.

There is a large fish swiftly chasing a group of tiny minnows, which dart away in all directions. Crawling along the shallow bottom and perched on the stalks of the water plants are snails of different sizes. If you look closely, you can also see round little worms, no longer than the end of your finger.

We could spend hours watching these interesting animals and plants. But we are after stranger game. And our game is far smaller. The creatures that we seek are so small that we cannot even see them. When we get home, we will need a microscope to watch them.

To capture the creatures, take one of your jars and skim some water from the top of the pond. Now take another jar and scoop out some water and mud from the bottom of the pond. This is all that needs to be done. Now let's see what we have caught.

A Circus Full of Life

WE ARE ABOUT TO PEEK into a very different world—a world that was discovered about three hundred years ago. In those days microscopes were new, and they were not very good. But a Dutchman named Antony van Leeuwenhoek learned how to polish lenses and put them in frames to make small hand microscopes. As time passed, he became more and more interested in his hobby. He would spend days and even weeks, polishing away on one tiny lens until he had it perfect. Then he would slip it into one of his small brass frames and examine all sorts of things with it.

Leeuwenhoek grew more and more excited at the things he saw. Through his tiny lenses, some no bigger than the head of a pin, he saw things smaller than anyone had ever seen before. He looked at little fleas

Drawing of Leeuwenhoek using his microscope. Eric Fraser.

and saw even smaller creatures crawling on their backs. He watched the blood flowing in fine blood vessels in a tadpole's tail. He spent many hours studying hair and skin and even scrapings from his own teeth.

But Leeuwenhoek's greatest surprise came one day when he looked through one of his wondrous lenses at a drop of rain water that had stood for a few days in a pot in his garden. Here he discovered a new world. In a single drop of water, he saw a circus full of life.

He saw clear little globs, which poked out little "horns" as they moved along. He peered at slipper-shaped creatures gliding through the water, swimming along with the help of many tiny "feet". He saw some "little beasts" that zipped by so fast and were so small that he could not tell just what they looked like. Sometimes they would stand still, and sometimes they would spin about like a top.

Leeuwenhoek learned that he could grow these small creatures in pepper water. They grew so well that he was able to see many thousands of these "animalcules" or little animals in a single drop of pepper water.

For nearly fifty years this Dutchman gazed through his many microscopes at his busy little worlds. He was so excited that he told everyone about his discoveries. He told his friends. He told the shopkeepers of the town. He told the officials at the town hall. And everyone came to his house to look through his microscopes.

But most important of all, he wrote letters to a famous group of scientists, members of the Royal Society of London, telling them of the small creatures he had seen.

These scientists were so amazed that at first they did not believe him. But after a time they saw this tiny world for themselves and recognized Leeuwenhoek as a fine scientist.

Now we are about to explore the world that Leeuwenhoek discovered nearly three hundred years ago.

The Amoeba:
a Living Glob

TO SEE WHAT KINDS of small creatures live in a pond, we too must look at a drop of water under a microscope. First we'll try the water that we scooped up from the bottom of the pond. The mud and leaves have settled, and the water is now clear. One drop of the clear water goes under the lens, and we find that it is swarming with life. Tiny creatures of different sizes and shapes are busily swimming to and fro. Little balls and rods and hooks wiggle and dart about.

The mud on the bottom, when we examine it under a lens, is also dotted with all sorts of queer bits of life. Pincushions on thin sticks send tiny tentacles out into the water and sometimes catch hold of the green or pink or purple "beasts" swimming by. Bright blue-green trumpet-shaped objects grow up from thin stalks.

All about them the water streams into their open tops, as though it were flowing into a funnel. Sometimes they seem to grow tired of drawing water in and blow it out instead. These queer creatures may curl up and disappear into their hollow stalks if they are disturbed. Or they may even break loose and swim away.

This is the strange jungle to be found at the bottom of the pond. And all the "beasts" of this strange world are so small that we would not know they were there if we did not have a microscope.

The most famous of all of these creatures is the *Amoeba*. It lurks on the bottoms of ponds and under rocks, and crawls along the stalks and leaves of water plants.

Amoeba Proteus, *photographed in oblique light.*
Courtesy Carolina Biological Supply Company.

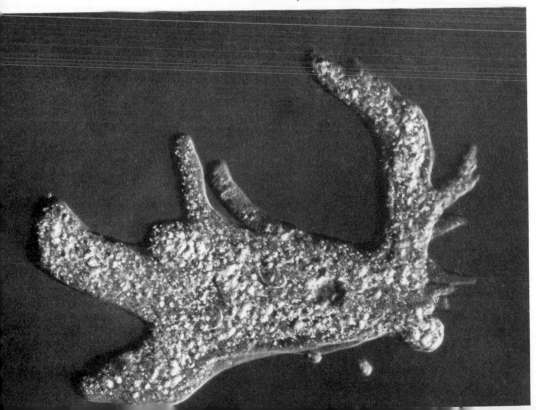

When you first look at an Amoeba, it seems hard to believe that this creature could be alive. It looks like a shapeless blob of jelly. It is so light colored that you can hardly see it. The Amoeba has no head, no real arms or legs or tail. You can see right into its body, as thought it were made of glass. And there seems to be very little to see! The Amoeba has no eyes, no ears, no mouth, no stomach, no heart, and no lungs. The whole Amoeba is just a single cell. (Our bodies are made of trillions of the little units called cells.) All that you can see inside the Amoeba are some little round spots, one larger one called the *nucleus,* one clear one filled with water, and some that seem to be filled with bits of food.

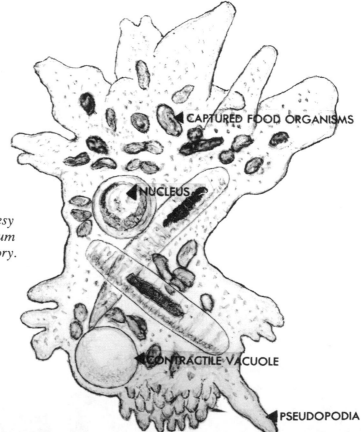

Diagram of an Amoeba. *Courtesy American Museum of Natural History.*

CAPTURED FOOD ORGANISMS

NUCLEUS

CONTRACTILE VACUOLE

PSEUDOPODIA

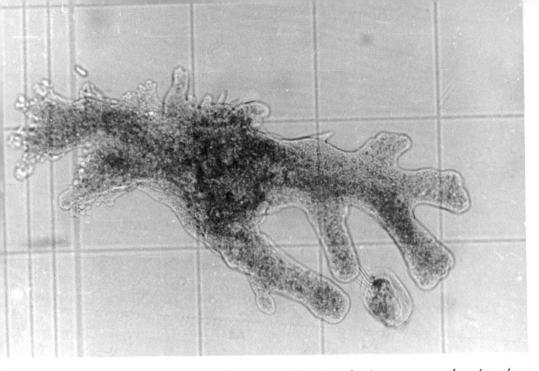

An Amoeba *about to catch a ciliate. The* Amoeba *is on a squared surface for measuring. The large squares are 1/100 of an inch on a side. Photo by Ralph Buchsbaum.*

With no arms or legs and no mouth, it is hard to imagine how an Amoeba catches its food and how it eats. Yet even without eyes to see, it knows when something good to eat is nearby. Perhaps it is a slipper-shaped Paramecium swimming by. Or some round ball-like creature, zipping along with lashes of a whip-like tail. There are many creatures in the pond even smaller than the Amoeba. In fact, even some pond animals whose bodies are made of many cells are small enough for an Amoeba to eat. For its one cell is a very large cell indeed.

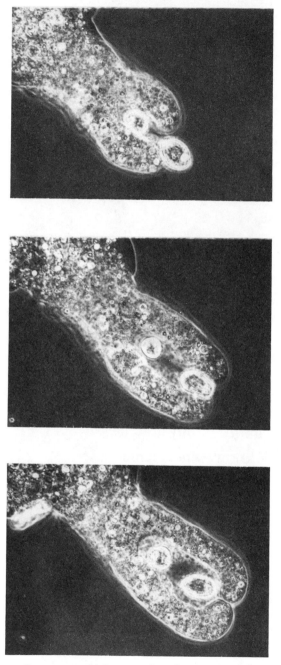

Many of the animals that an Amoeba stalks in its mud jungle at the bottom of the pond can swim quickly through the water. But their speed cannot always help them to escape. Creeping along, slow but sure, the globlike hunter sends out what look like little arms or legs from the jelly of its body. These are called *pseudopods,* a word that means "false feet". Soon some of the Amoeba's pseudopods are wrapped around its prey, and then the whole Amoeba seems to flow right around its helpless victim. Though the prey may try to swim away, it cannot escape. Soon it is a tasty meal, wrapped up in a little round package called a *food vacuole* inside the Amoeba's body.

Sequence of pictures showing an Amoeba *swallowing a* Tetrahymena. *Photo by Dr. David M. Prescott.*

An Amoeba never has a chance to grow old. Each individual Amoeba lives just a day or so. And yet, unless it is eaten by some larger animal, or its watery home suddenly dries up or freezes over, it will never die. For when an Amoeba is big and fat enough, a strange thing happens. It splits in half! Instead of one Amoeba, there are two. Each is a perfect half-size copy of the mother. But where *is* the mother? She is gone, but she lives on in her two "daughters". They creep along just as their mother did before them. If they can find enough food and do not get eaten themselves, they too will grow fat and split in two, just as their mother did.

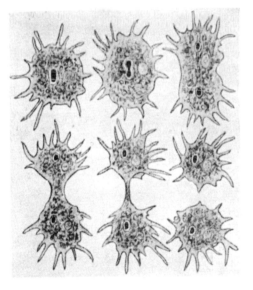

Amoeba *showing changes that take place during division. Courtesy American Museum of Natural History.*

The Amoeba must always have water in which to live. It can crawl about in a pond, or even in a mud puddle made by a rainfall. But when the water dries up, the Amoeba need not die. For these creatures can curl up into tiny, tough "sleeping bags" called *cysts*. The cysts of Amoebas and other pond animals can be carried by the wind for great distances through the air. And if they land once more in water, they will come to life again.

Paramecium:
a Slipper That Swims

THE AMOEBA AND THE OTHER creatures we have seen live in the water and mud at the bottom of the pond. What lives at the top of the pond? To find this out, we must look at the other jar.

When a drop of this water is put under a microscope, we can see many creatures swimming about, most of them even smaller than the Amoeba. But they are quite different. Most of them have a special shape all their own, which does not change as the Amoeba's does. And they move more quickly. Many of these creatures are built for speed. They have smooth fishlike shapes. And they paddle along with rows of tiny "oars", which are called *cilia*.

One of these animals is the *Paramecium*. It looks like a miniature slipper. But it is a slipper that swims.

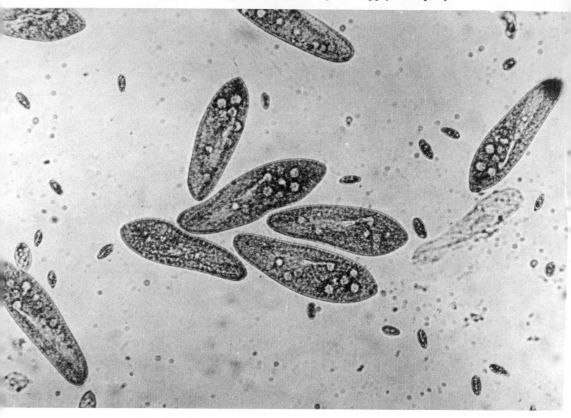

Its body is covered all over with short, hairlike cilia. These cilia move back and forth in a beautiful rhythm, and send the Paramecium gracefully gliding through the water.

Like the Amoeba, the Paramecium has no head or arms or legs. But it does have a "mouth" right in the middle of its body. We can see into the Paramecium's body. If you remember, the Amoeba had a nucleus. But the Paramecium has two nuclei, a big one and a small one. In addition, there is a large round clear spot at each end, surrounded by what looks like many tiny petals. These daisylike structures, called *contractile vacuoles,* help the Paramecium get rid of its extra water. Other spots, food vacuoles, are moving "stomachs" where the Paramecium digests its food.

In some ways Paramecia are built like the men-of-war that roamed the seas a few hundred years ago. These mighty ships had rows of guns along their sides. The Paramecium has a set of "guns" too. It can shoot out tiny threadlike darts from small "portholes" between its cilia. Some of these darts are sticky and help to anchor the Paramecium while it is feeding upon even smaller creatures called bacteria. (Its cilia swirl them into its mouth, and then into its body.) Some of the darts are poison-tipped. These are defense weapons. The Paramecium shoots them at enemies that are trying to eat it.

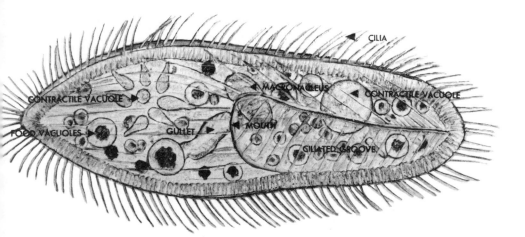

Diagram showing the principal parts of the Paramecium.
Courtesy American Museum of Natural History.

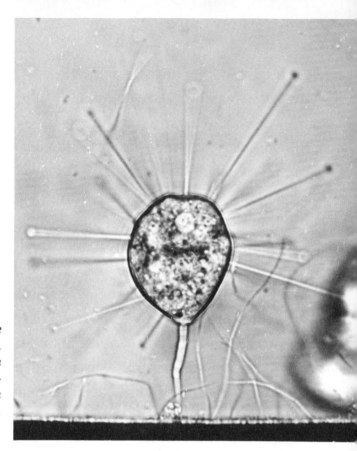

A living, adult Suctorian. *The upper tentacles capture prey. The heavier one at the bottom is the stalk that holds the* Suctorian *to a surface. Photograph courtesy Dr. Ruth V. Dippell.*

There are many little monsters in the pond that love to eat these small slippers. Giant Amoebas may surround them and swallow them whole. But some enemies are even smaller than the Paramecium itself.

Paramecia must be careful as they swim along. For lurking on the water plants and rocks may be *Suctorians,* greedy little monsters that look like pincushions mounted on long, thin sticks. The "pins" sticking out of their bodies are tentacles. With them, the Suctorians can grab and hold swimming creatures like Paramecium, and suck the life from them.

Other enemies have rows of cilia and can swim quickly after a passing Paramecium. The little *Didinium* is one of these. A whole Paramecium can be swallowed by a Didinium only half its size. The swift little Didinium sends out a tube that catches hold of the Paramecium. Then the Didinium's body seems to stretch right over the Paramecium like a mitten. Soon all of the Paramecium is stuffed inside.

The slipper animals are fun to watch as they swim through the water. As they glide along, they turn slowly about like a top. If a Paramecium bumps into something, a weed or a ribbon of algae, it will stop short. Then it will back away, turn slightly to one side, and try again. The Paramecium is not very smart. It

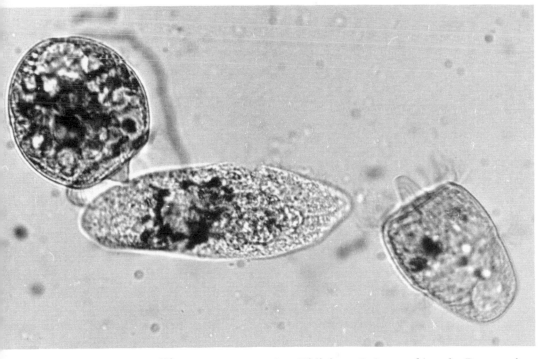

The upper creature is a Didinium. *It is attacking the* Paramecium. *The* Didinium *will paralyze the* Paramecium *and consume it within three minutes. Photograph courtesy Dr. Ruth V. Dippell.*

always turns exactly the same amount. On its new try it may bump again, on a new part of the weed or algae, completely missing an escape hole in between. But it will try again and again, until it finally finds a way out.

After about a day of living and growing, the Paramecium gives birth to two daughters, just like itself. It splits in half just as the Amoeba did. But when a Paramecium meets another Paramecium, something strange may happen. They will stay very close together until their bodies are actually joined by a little bridge. Each Paramecium now has two small nuclei, and it gives one of them to the other Paramecium. This is called *conjugation*.

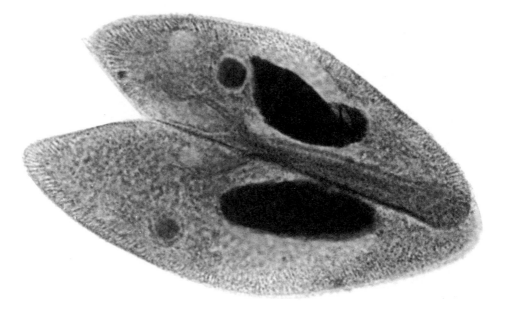

Paramecium *conjugation. Courtesy Carolina Biological Supply Company.*

For a time the two Paramecia stay close together. But after a while they move apart. Then each will divide, and divide again. This time there are four daughters from each mother cell. These new Paramecia will eat and grow and swim about, and soon they will be mothers too.

Many other small pond creatures also have cilia and are related to the Paramecium. There are thousands of different kinds, with different shapes and colors. Some live on the bottom, and others swim near the top. Some, like the trumpet-shaped *Stentors*, build slender tubes, attached to some solid object, in which they can

A group of Stentor.
Photo by Ralph Buchsbaum.

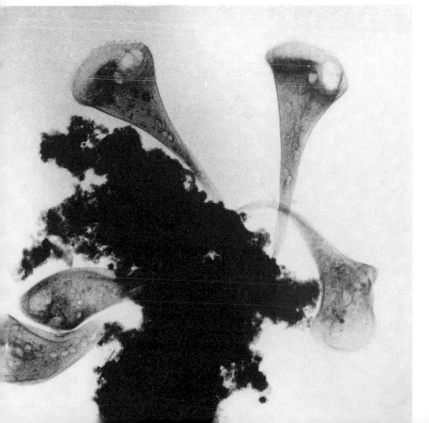

A living Stentor *photographed in oblique light.*
Courtesy Carolina Biological Supply Company.

hide. They use their cilia mainly to swirl in food from the pond water. Others, like the oval-shaped pink *Blepharismas,* have bands of cilia over their bodies, which help them swim swiftly about. Even the Suctorians are relatives of the Paramecium. For when they are young, they have cilia, too. They lose them as they grow older.

Algae:
the Green Blanket

REMEMBER THE THIN GREEN COVER spread across the pond? We have some of this very same pond scum in our second jar. It has creatures in it, too. If we look at a bit of this green scum under the microscope, we see many long green ribbons, tangled together. Floating

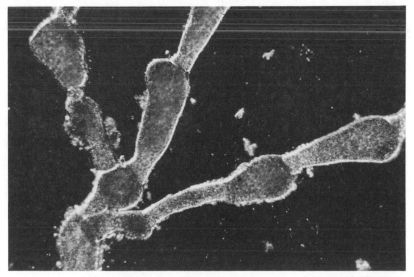

Algae. Courtesy American Museum of Natural History.

among them, here and there, are little green balls of different sizes. These are the plants of the microscopic world. These single green cells and chains of cells are called *algae*. Like the plants of the world we see every day, these algae do not eat. They drink in the energy of the sunlight and make their own food. Some of this food they may store away to use at night or when the sun is covered by clouds.

The little green balls and clumps of balls that float about near the top of the pond are called *Chlorella*. Each little ball is a single cell, like the Amoeba or the Paramecium. Like them it has a nucleus. But it also has a green substance called *chlorophyll*. It is this green chemical that helps Chlorella and the other green plants of the world capture energy from sunlight and make their own food. Unlike the Amoeba and Paramecium, Chlorella cannot move by itself. It just floats along in the water of the pond.

Scientists have been experimenting with Chlorella for years. They think it could make a cheap source of food to help feed the hungry people of the world. Scientists also believe that Chlorella could be grown on spaceships, to provide food for the astronauts and help keep the air pure. For when green plants like Chlorella make food, they give off oxygen, which we and other animals need to breathe. And they take in the carbon dioxide that we breathe out.

The alga, Spirogyra. *Photo by P. S. Tice. Courtesy Ralph Buchsbaum.*

Other algae, called *Spirogyra,* look like long green ribbons at first glance. You can even see them without a microscope. But if you look at them more closely under a microscope, you will see that they are more like long trains of many cars, all alike. Each of these "cars" is a single cell. And when you look very closely, you will see that the whole cell is not green. Instead there is a thin green ribbon of chlorophyll, coiled around and around like the stripes on a barber pole.

You can see for yourself how Spirogyra make more of themselves. Take one of the long green strands and tear it into many smaller pieces with a sharp pin. Then leave it in pond water for a few days on a sunlit windowsill. You will find that each day the small pieces grow longer. Soon each one will be as long as the first strand. The cells have divided to make more cells.

Spirogyra have another way of reproducing. They can conjugate, much like the Paramecium. Two whole strands line up side by side. Little tubes form between each pair of cells, so that the strands look like a green ladder. Now all the inside of each cell in one strand flows through its tube into its partner cell on the other strand. Only empty walls remain in one set of cells. In the cells of the other strand, the pairs have joined to form tough new cells called *spores*. These spores are

Spirogyra *conjugation. Courtesy Carolina Biological Supply Company.*

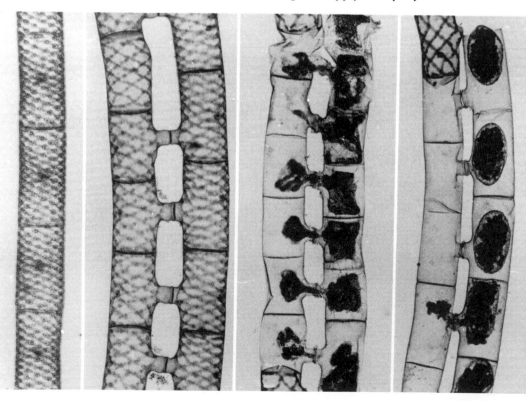

Dasya, *a type of marine algae. Courtesy Carolina Biological Supply Company.*

usually formed when the pond is drying up, or when cold weather is coming and the pond may soon freeze over. The walls of the strand break apart, and the little spores sink to the bottom. There they "sleep" until good weather comes again. Then each spore can form a new strand of Spirogyra.

Other strandlike algae grow in branches, and some even form green nets that spread over the water. These strandlike algae are all made up of large numbers of cells, grouped together in colonies. But each cell of a strand is like every other cell; they do not work together as the many different cells of our bodies do.

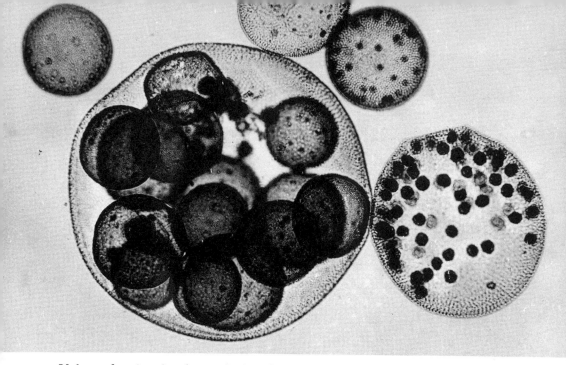

Volvox showing daughter colonies. Courtesy Carolina Biological Supply Company.

In another type of algae called *Volvox*, colonies of cells are grouped together in a different way. Instead of long strands, the cells form a hollow ball. Each cell has two long, whiplike tails called *flagella*. As they lash back and forth, the whole ball turns slowly in the water.

Sometimes cells break away from the wall of the ball and float inside. There they divide and multiply many times to form new, smaller hollow balls. At last the parent ball bursts open, and the smaller daughter colonies float out into the pond to take up life on their own.

Euglena: Is it a Plant or an Animal?

SWIMMING QUICKLY AMONG the algae, darting in and out of the tangled "weeds", are many tiny animals. The Paramecium is here. So is the hungry Didinium, trying to catch a Paramecium for its dinner. These and other small animals are busily moving about, chasing after one another, or gobbling the floating algae.

But if we look closely, we will see other moving creatures. They dart about, propelled by long lashing tails. Some of these are the *Euglenas*. Each one has a single thin, whiplike tail, called a *flagellum*. Its tail may be longer than its body. The Euglena can also move by changing from a long fishlike shape to a plump pear shape, then back again. It has a red "eye-spot", which can see light. Euglenas will always swim toward sunlight that is just bright enough. They will

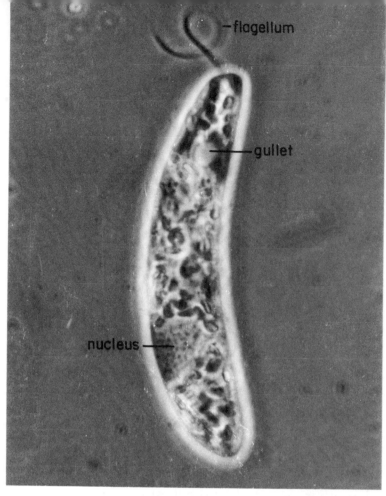

Euglena, *stained to show flagellum. Courtesy J. J. Wolken.*

swim away from places that are too bright or too dark. They seem to be animals like the other moving creatures.

But a second look shows that these "animals" have many bits of green chlorophyll inside their bodies, just like some of the algae. And if we watch them carefully, we will not see them eat at all. They can make their own food. In this way they are like plants.

Euglenas are strange in-between creatures. Some scientists call them animals. Other scientists say they are plants.

Trees are plants. So are flowers and grass and the weeds that grow in the pond. They are all green and make their own food. But they do not move about from place to place by themselves.

Dogs and cats and people are animals. So are birds and fish and frogs. They all move about freely. But they cannot make their own food. They must eat other animals or plants.

So the Euglena is something like each of these groups. It moves around like an animal. But it makes its own food like a plant. If a Euglena is kept in the dark for a while, its green spots will disappear. Then it cannot make its own food. A colorless Euglena must be fed, or it will die. But if it is put back in the sunlight, its green spots will soon come back.

Some scientists say that it can never be decided whether the Euglena is a plant or an animal. And we should not even try. These scientists place Euglena in a group of "in-between" creatures called *protists*.

Rotifers:
Animals with Wheels

ALL THE ANIMALS THAT we have looked at so far have been made of just a single cell. But this single cell could move, could catch its food, and could grow and give birth to young.

Yet in any drop of pond water we might find other animals, just as small, but made up of many cells—hundreds or even a thousand of them. These are the *rotifers*. And what strange creatures they are! They squeeze in and out like accordions. On the tops of their heads are one or two whirling wheels—circles of cilia that beat in such perfect rhythm that they seem to spin about. These "wheels" sweep in water filled with bits of food.

Rotifers are no bigger than Paramecia, but they are far more complicated. A rotifer has a tiny brain, one or two eyes, a mouth, a stomach, and a throat with "teeth" in it, which help to grind up the rotifer's food. And outside, in addition to the "wheels", rotifers have toes with sticky ends, with which they can stick to a stone, a stem, or some other object. Some rotifers spend nearly all their lives attached to some object in a pond. Others swim through the water, propelled by their whirling wheels of cilia, or creep along the bottom, holding on with their heads and toes.

Some rotifers like to live together. A group of them will hold onto each other with their sticky toes. Such groups may swim through the water like a big turning ball.

Rotifer: Philodina. *Photo by Dr. Norman Meadow.*

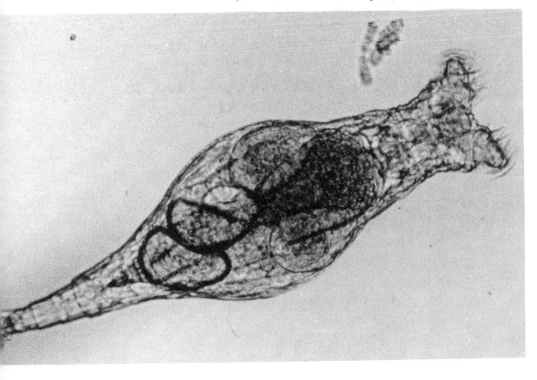

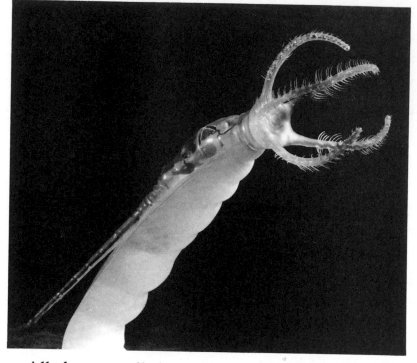

All the one-celled pond creatures "give birth" by simply splitting in two. But the rotifer actually lays eggs, which soon hatch into young rotifers. And in time each rotifer will grow old and die. Some kinds of rotifers live for less than a week, others for a month or more.

Through most of the warm season, all the rotifers in a pond are females. They grow and reproduce all by themselves. There are no males to be found. But toward the end of the season, when the weather is getting cooler, the mother rotifers lay special small eggs that hatch into males. The males swim about and mate with females, and now a new type of egg is laid. They have tough, thick walls around them and will not hatch for a long time. These are winter eggs; and while the pond is covered with ice, they lie at the bottom, safe and protected. When spring comes again, these tough little eggs hatch out into female rotifers, which will soon be mothers themselves.

Rotifers live in all the fresh waters of the world. You would hardly ever find a lake, or a pond, or even a mud puddle without some of these wheeled animals in it. But if a puddle or pond dries up, the rotifers curl up into cysts, just as the one-celled pond animals do. They can stay asleep this way for years. The tiny cysts are so light that the wind may carry them for miles and miles. But if these cysts fall into some water—a lake, or pond, another puddle, or even an open jar of water on your windowsill—they come back to life.

The Hydra:
a Tentacled Monster

MANY OF THE ANIMALS we have looked at are so small that we cannot see them at all with our own eyes. Others are just barely large enough to be seen as tiny specks, if we hold our jars of water up to the sunlight. But these jars of water also contain larger animals. To our eyes, they may look like tiny threads. Yet if we look at them under a microscope, suddenly the tiny threads are transformed into slim monsters, with a crown of waving tentacles.

These are *hydras*. Their name comes from an ancient Greek legend. Once, so the story goes, there was a deadly monster called the Hydra, which was a serpent with many heads, each attached to a long neck like a waving tentacle. If one of its heads was chopped off, two more grew back in its place. The hydra in the pond is not quite like the Hydra of the ancient Greeks. If it loses one of its tentacles, only one new one will grow back in its place.

To smaller creatures in the pond, the hydra is just as dangerous as its ancient namesake. For its tentacles are armed with deadly weapons. Some are like tiny lassoes, which can wrap around a prey and hold it tightly. Others are like sticky threads, which tangle and cling to a victim. Still other weapons are like poisoned dart guns.

If a Paramecium or rotifer or some other small pond animal is unlucky enough to brush against a hydra's

Hydra. *Courtesy Carolina Biological Supply Company.*

tentacle, the creature may be instantly speared, lassoed, and bound. Then the other tentacles will bend in and wrap around the victim. Slowly they will pull it into the hydra's mouth, which is right in the middle of the circle of tentacles.

When the hydra has finished digesting its meal, the waste products pass out into the water through its mouth. For that is the only opening its body has.

Nearly all the tiny animals of the pond may fall prey to the hydra. These tentacled hunters gobble down any one-celled creatures that happen to brush by them. They also feed on rotifers, on small water worms, and on tiny *crustaceans,* relatives of shrimps and crabs, as well. One of the most common of these little pond crustaceans is the water flea. This is not really a flea. It

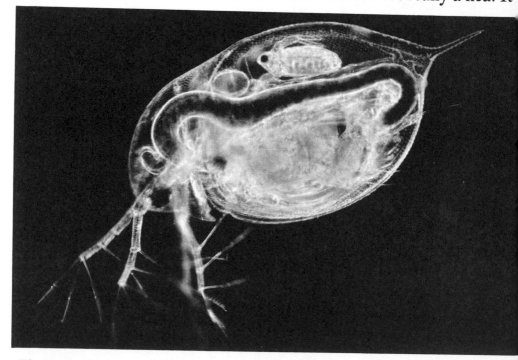

The water flea or Daphnia. *This is a female with unborn young. Photo by P. S. Tice. Courtesy Ralph Buchsbaum.*

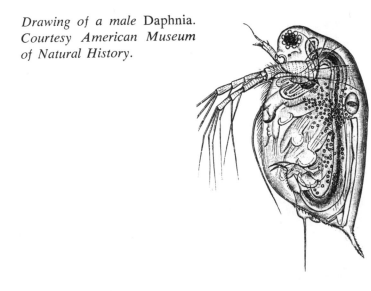

Drawing of a male Daphnia.
*Courtesy American Museum
of Natural History.*

looks rather like a plump little chicken with feathery legs on top of its head. It swims about in jerks, like the hops of a flea. But if it happens to bump into a hydra, it is soon caught and eaten.

Sometimes a hydra gobbles its food so quickly that it swallows one of its own tentacles! But this does not seem to harm it. It does not digest its own body cells. Soon its mouth opens and its tentacle slips out.

A hydra usually spends most of its time attached to the bottom of the pond or to a rock or stalk of a plant. For the bottom or base of the hydra's slender body is sticky, much like the foot of the rotifer. But sometimes not enough food passes the place where the hydra has settled. Then it will start to wave its tentacles about. This stirs up the water and may bring in some food.

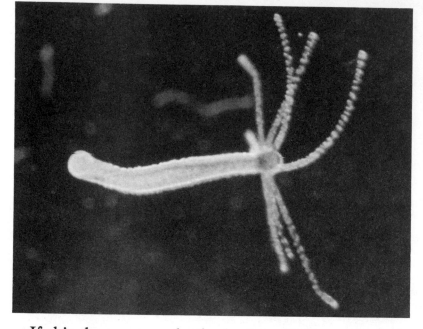

If this does not work, the hydra will move away. It may move along very slowly, gliding along on its base. Or, if it is in more of a hurry, it can move much faster by turning somersaults. First it bends over and grasps the bottom of the pond (or rock or stalk of a plant) with its tentacles. When it has a firm hold, it lets go with its base and flips over. Then the base bends down and takes hold in a new place, and the tentacles let go. The hydra straightens up and begins all over again.

In a drop of water we can also often find a hydra with what looks like a baby hydra growing out of its side. And this is exactly what it is. For most hydras give birth to young by a process called budding. First a little bump appears on the parent hydra's side. The bump grows larger. Soon small tentacles begin to sprout. The

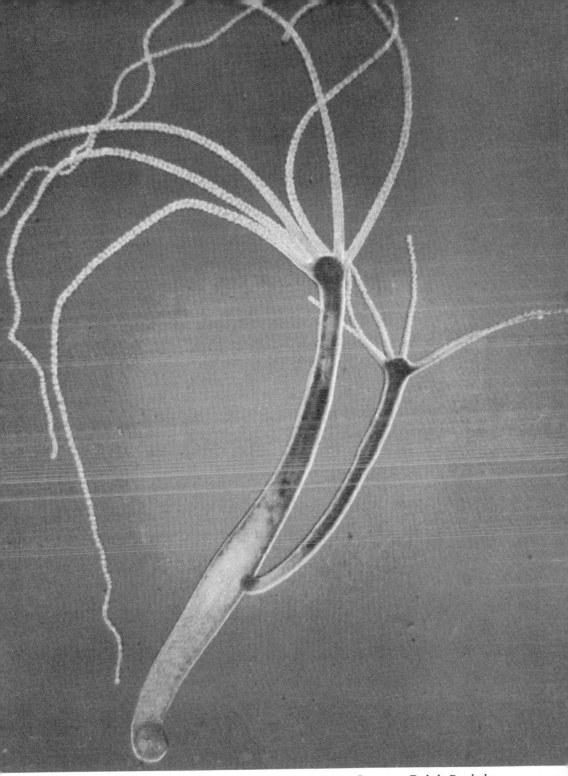

Hydra *with bud. Photo by P. S. Tice. Courtesy Ralph Buchsbaum.*

baby grows as a perfect but smaller copy of its parent. At last it breaks away and drifts off to settle down and live a life of its own.

Hydras can also mate. The male can somehow sense when a female is nearby. Then tiny sperm cells with lashing flagella swim out of special openings in his body and through the water to the female. There they join with eggs in her body. Soon she lays her eggs, which will grow into new hydras.

The Flatworm:
a Gliding Ribbon

ALTHOUGH WE'VE ALREADY found many interesting creatures in water from the pond—slippers that swim, living globs, animals with wheels or tentacles on their heads—there are still more. There are ribbons that glide, for example. Their dull-colored bodies blend into the mud of the bottom of the pond so well that it is hard to see them at first. But it is possible to catch some of them for a better look.

First we must cut a little piece of raw liver or some other fresh meat, tie a string around it, and dangle it into the jar of water from the bottom of the pond. We have to hold the meat so that it touches one side of the jar. In a few minutes tiny ribbon-like creatures come gliding up the side of the jar. Soon they are clinging to the meat.

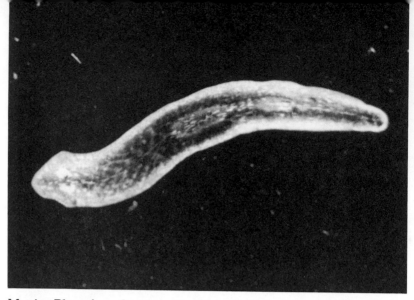

Moving Planarian. *Courtesy Carolina Biological Supply Company.*

Under a magnifying glass or microscope, these little ribbon-like animals appear to be flat little worms (scientists call them *Planarians*). Each has a long, slim body and a head shaped like a triangle. In the middle of the head are two dark eyes, looking up. The flatworm's eyes are not as good as ours. They do not see clearly at all. In fact, what they mainly see is light, shining down at them.

Flatworms do not like the light. They spend most of their time hiding under rocks or the leaves of plants. If light shines upon them, they move away.

Planarians have a rather strange way of moving. On the underside of their bodies they make a kind of slime, which flows under them. This is like the slippery trail that a snail leaves behind it. But a flatworm actually "swims" in its trail of slime. For the underside of its body is covered with many rows of cilia, tiny hairlike "oars", which beat back and forth. These cilia are very much like the cilia of the Paramecium and its relatives. As the cilia beat backward, they send the flatworm gliding forward.

The Planarian also has another, faster way to move. It has muscles, just as we do, that help it to bend and twist, and hump itself along.

A flatworm's head not only has eyes that can sense light, but also has special cells that can tell when food is nearby in the water. The food may be a small water animal or a bit of decaying matter, such as the remains of a dead fish. As soon as the worm senses that there is food in the water nearby, it begins to move toward it. It catches its prey by humping its body over the food and pressing it down against the bottom of the pond or stone.

When a Planarian is about to eat, a hollow tube comes out of its mouth and sucks at the food until it is broken into small pieces. These bits pass down the tube. Inside the worm's body they are caught by cells that look and act something like tiny Amoebas. The bits of food are neatly wrapped up and stored away in food vacuoles. Bits that cannot be digested pass out again through the mouth. For like the hydra, the flatworm has only one opening to its digestive system.

But the flatworm does have other openings in its body. Many pairs of tiny holes may be found along its back. These carry water out of the worm's body. The water is sent out by little bulb-shaped cells called *flame cells*. Inside each cell there is a group of cilia, beating back and forth like the flickering of a flame.

Planarians have several ways of making more of themselves. All your friends are either boys or girls. And all the adults you know are either men or women. But each flatworm is *both* male and female. Yet a flatworm cannot have babies by itself. Two of them must mate. After they mate, *both* of them lay eggs, which hatch into baby flatworms.

Planarians have another even odder way of reproducing. Sometimes the body of one of these worms seems to pinch in at the middle. Then suddenly the two halves struggle to pull apart. The tail end holds tight to the bottom of the pond, while the head end tries to wriggle forward. It is like a tug of war. The worm's body stretches out in the middle, thinner and thinner, until it finally snaps. Then the two halves crawl away to lead their own lives. Soon the head half grows a new tail, and the tail half grows a new head!

The growth of new body parts to replace ones that have been lost is called *regeneration*. Scientists have long wondered why some animals, such as hydras and flatworms, can regenerate lost parts, while others, like

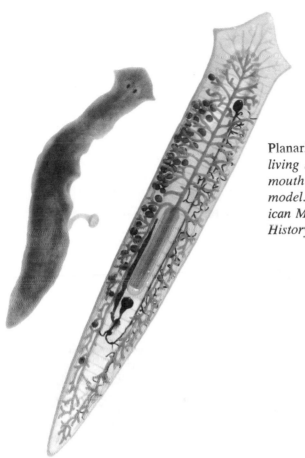

Planaria maculata—*a living specimen showing mouth tube, and a glass model. Courtesy American Museum of Natural History.*

dogs and horses and people, cannot. They have tried many different experiments on flatworms, hoping to learn more about this mysterious process.

If a flatworm is cut in half, separating the head from the tail, then the tail half will grow a new head, and the head half will grow a new tail. If a piece is cut out from the middle, it can grow a new head *and* a new tail. If a flatworm is cut down the middle, each side will regenerate the missing side. But if the cut is carefully made only partway, separating one half of the head from the other but leaving them both attached to the body, something very strange happens. Each half head grows a new half, and soon the worm becomes a two-headed worm. One of these worms is very odd to watch. For often the heads seem to be trying to move in opposite directions.

A two-headed Planaria. *Photo by Ralph Buchsbaum.*

Flatworms can be kept as pets. They need a dish with pond water that is changed every few days, and some mud and stones, and perhaps a few plants. They should be fed a bit of raw meat every now and then, although if they are not fed for a while, they will be all right; for these worms can store food in their bodies. If they have nothing new to eat, they can live on their stored food for a month or more. But each day they get smaller and smaller.

A World
in a Drop of Water

WHILE WE ARE AT WORK and play in our big world, there are many unseen worlds all about us. The creatures we have already seen are some of the ones that live in a drop of pond water. We have watched them being born, living, eating, fighting and dying. But we have looked at only a very small part of this world. There are thousands of different kinds of creatures that may live in the water of a pond, each too small to see clearly without a magnifying glass or microscope. And in the waters of the seas there are many thousands more.

Many of the microscopic creatures are made of only a single cell. There are different kinds of Amoebas. Many have soft, jelly-like bodies, and creep along on pseudopods. But some of the relatives of the Amoeba that live in the sea have hard shells about them. Through tiny holes in their shells they send out pseudopods like tentacles to catch their prey.

The Paramecium, too, has many relatives. They all have cilia, at least at some time in their lives. Some of these tiny animals swim about, with cilia all over their bodies. Others have cilia only around their mouths, which help them to feed. The cilia of some of these

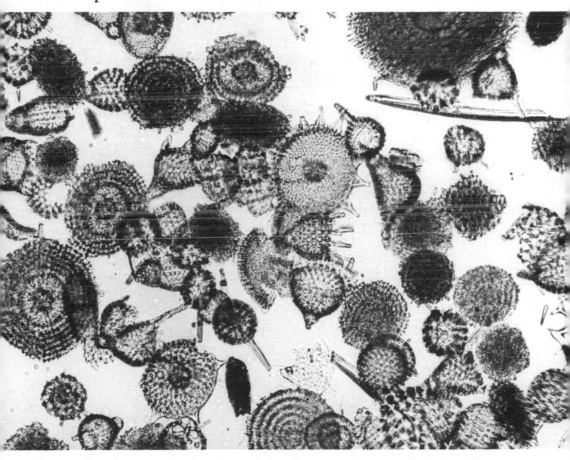

Shelled Amoebas *of the sea*—Radiolaria. *Courtesy Carolina Biological Supply Company.*

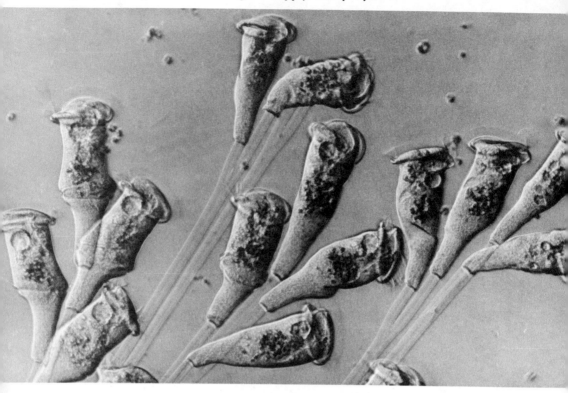

creatures grow together in stiff clumps. They may use them like little feet, to crawl about on the bottom of a pond instead of swimming.

Many one-celled creatures of ponds and seas have flagella, like the Euglena. Some of these have no chlorophyll and are considered to be animals. But others seem to be plants. Some of them are covered with tiny crystal shells, as complicated and varied as snowflakes.

Not all the one-celled water plants of the world are green like Chlorella and Spirogyra. Some algae are blue-green, or golden brown, or a bright red that seems to stain the seas with blood. Many of these have chemicals that are not chlorophyll, but work in very much the same way to help them make their own food.

The waters of ponds and seas also swarm with small many-celled animals. There are more than a thousand different kinds of rotifers, many no larger than a Paramecium. In the same ponds and streams may often be found other tiny animals, called *Gastrotrichs*. These are about the same size as rotifers, and look very much like them. But they have no crown of "wheels" on their

A living Gastrotrich. Courtesy Carolina Biological Supply Company.

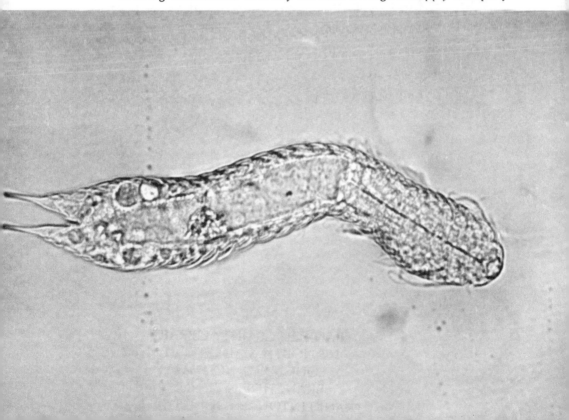

heads. Instead, their cilia are on the underside of their bodies, like those of a flatworm. The Gastrotrichs use their cilia to swim.

Worms of many kinds can be found, both in fresh water and in oceans. There are flatworms that crawl along like slender ribbons. There are tiny wriggling roundworms. And there are even minute relatives of the earthworm, whose bodies are made of a long series of segments or rings.

Many different kinds of small crustaceans, such as the little water flea, also swim about in ponds and seas. And some of the tiny animals that swim about are young forms, or *larvae,* which will not be microscopic when they are fully grown. A small bean-shaped creature, swimming about with cilia, might be the larva of a kind of jellyfish. Another might grow up to be a starfish. These larvae go through an amazing series of changes as they grow, just as a caterpillar changes into a butterfly and a tadpole into a frog.

What a wonderful new world of life Leeuwenhoek discovered. And if you have a microscope, or can borrow one, you too can be an explorer in this strange unseen world.

Index